ATOMS & ORCHESTRAS

The Case for Standards-Based Management

Derrick Van Mell

Tranton Press Books

Cover design by Broadbent & Williams
Interior layout by First Person Productions
Image credits on page 74

ISBN 9780977091447

Tranton Press Books
P.O.Box 6554
Madison, WI 53716

To Ron Jarek,
a great boss who saved me

The Center's simple tools and careful facilitation got us moving. We'd been trying to do too much. Our first Projects Summary showed we'd overcommitted ourselves. Our new 1-page Goal Tree clarified priorities and unlocked energy to focus on the big picture.

– Bob Wahlin,
President,
Stoughton Trailers

The Management Self-Audit provided extraordinary results. After an hour's training, our team spotted gaps and strengths and agreed quickly on what to prioritize. The Index gave me and the board confidence nothing was overlooked. The conversation helped everyone see how everyone connects and contributes.

– Ruth Schmidt,
Executive Director,
WECA

I'd used The Center of Management Terms & Practices' Index to conduct our planning, so I was happy to participate in one of their local seminars on its Toolkit. I've rarely seen 30 executives as engaged! It's now a tool we use to help us quickly understand our real priorities: our sales closing rate took a big step up.

– Ed Purcell,
President,
Vertical Greenwalls

As a lawyer, I've used The Center's Toolkit for years and it's not only helped me as head of the office, but also improved my understanding of how my CEO clients think and of the language they use.

– Tim Stewart,
Managing Partner,
Dewitt Law Firm

The General Management Index helped me and other family business members have confidence we were covering all the issues and speaking the same language. The Goal Tree gave all of us powerful focus quickly.

– Jeff Lerdahl,
President,
Lerdahl Business Interiors

My Workgroup at The Center helped me craft the three 'Hard to Ask' questions that our management team used to make a really tough decision. The Workgroup peers listened carefully and gave me both the ideas and the confidence to lead this career-critical conversation."

– Susan Dineen,
Marketing Director,
ACS

About the Author

Before founding the Center for Management Terms & Practices in 2017, Derrick Van Mell was a management consultant for 25 years and worked with hundreds of managers and board members in all types and sizes of organizations. His specialty was planning major capital projects. Derrick has a BA in Economics, an MBA, and an MA in English. He's the author of dozens of published articles and the books *Buildings Matter* and *Question-Based Planning.* Derrick has spoken throughout the US and in Europe and Asia. His passion is helping people work together on something that makes the world a better place.

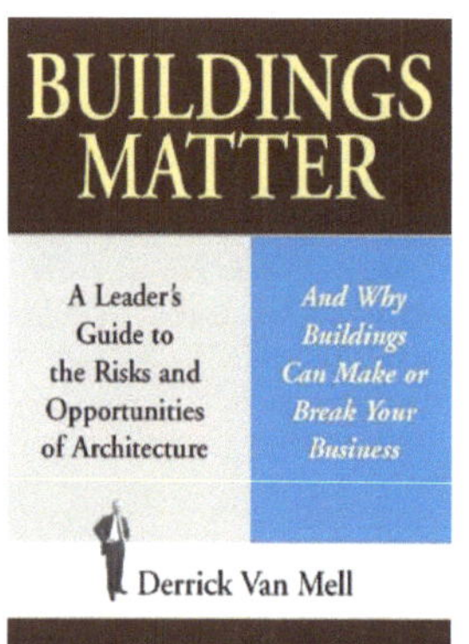

Acknowledgments

This book is built on the rich ideas, experiences, and passions of the members of The Center for Management Terms & Practices. Special thanks to the book's reviewers, particularly Jennifer Stangl of Exact Sciences, but also Al Antoniewicz, Brian Baker, Nathan Bares, Zach Blumenfeld, Stephen Barone, Bob DeVita, Susan Dineen, Brandon Gador, Mark Gale, Bryon Johnson, Bill Mitchell, Tom Oakley, Viva Valentine, Steve Johannsen, Kieran Sweeney, and Susan Van Mell. Long-time friends and collaborators, David Williams created the graphics and Sarah White provided editing and layout. Robert Van Mell was instrumental in developing The General Management Index as well as the case for Standards-Based Management. All the sins of omission and commission are on my head.

Contents at a Glance

Scan this code for PDFs of the parts of this book.

Chapter Contents

PART I
Overview & Orientation

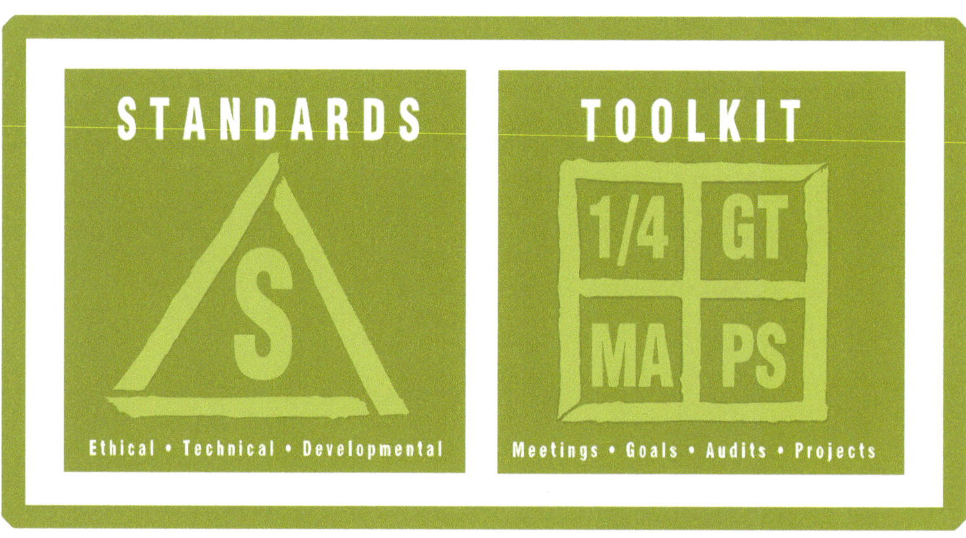

1 · A Cause and a Calling

If you're a manager, how would it feel to be trusted and admired by every employee and executive? If you're an executive—a manager of managers—what if you could delegate goals and projects with perfect confidence? How would your organization benefit by your giving it a reputation for having great managers?

This book is for managers with several years of experience who have chosen—or are considering—management as their career path or calling. These are people who care about their teams and simply put, want to be better bosses and are willing to work at it. This book will help them as they grow throughout their careers.

The personal rewards are immense. We've all had bad bosses, but I hope you've had a boss that helped you fulfill your potential and provided you with meaningful work in a trusting and collaborative culture. Having been a great manager is a career well spent.

Our cause is to help managers create safe, inclusive, and rewarding work for everyone.

Adopting the standard terms, tools, and practices gives managers a common language, which improves communication and builds a culture of trust and collaboration. Using standards creates transparency in setting priorities and making decisions. Transparency fosters inclusion and a feeling of ownership. Sharing a language is also essential to forging relationships up, down, and cross-functionally. Everyone wants to "be on the same page." Standards-Based Management is that page.

In this book, you'll also see the measurable benefits of applying management's ethical, technical, and developmental standards to a kit of four one-page tools.

Applying these standards through The General Management Toolkit creates a framework that substantially improves meetings, margins, and morale. Standards-Based Management blends science into the art of management.

You can read the chapters in this book in almost any order, but the first section is about the framework of general management's ethical, technical, and developmental **standards**. All the chapters end with ideas for individual and group activities and three good discussion questions.

Before closing with ideas for testing and implementing Standards-Based Management, Chapter 8 is about **the promise and rewards of service**. I hope you'll take up this challenge and opportunity.

Management ability is the best way to find and capitalize on growth opportunities for each employee and, through them, the organization.

Next chapter: We'll prove that standards can change the world.

Great Managers are Question Heroes

I was in a meeting helping a tech billionaire plan her next building. The topic was lighting, and the architect, engineer, lighting consultant, contractor, and I were engaged in the usual "dodgeball meeting," blasting each other with our ideas and dodging everybody else's. The client was tilted back in her chair next to me, saying nothing, scribbling in a small notebook.

After fifteen minutes, she leaned in to put her notebook in front of everyone. "I just want to understand the questions we're trying to answer. What about these three?" We peered at her questions and said, no, no, that's not right. She said "OK" and tilted back in her chair. She scratched out her list, and we went back to dodgeball. Fifteen more minutes go by and she leans in again: "How about these three questions?" We all said, "Yeah! That's right. That's what we're trying to answer!" and the meeting ended then and there. Off we went, full of confidence.

Two days later I'm walking down the street and then stopped like someone had hit me in the head with a two-by-four. I'd realized we never literally answered the questions, but we all knew just what to do.

A big theme of this book is how to be a question hero, the manager everyone counts on to ask just the right question at just the right time.

2 · Atoms and Orchestras: Two Standards That Changed the World

To prove the value of standards, let's time-travel to February 17, 1869, when Russian chemist Dimitri Mendeleyev had the most valuable idea anyone has ever had: the periodic table of elements. Without this structured standard, we wouldn't have iPhones, Tylenol, jet fuel, shrink wrap, fusion, or Netflix.

Atoms: The Periodic Table

The periodic table gave scientists and engineers a common language so they could collaborate on making blockbuster molecules. But Mendeleyev hadn't just cataloged the atoms: he'd peered into the inner workings of the physical universe and, through his understanding, built a foundation under the science of chemistry.

Starting in the upper left with Hydrogen, it first organizes the elements by row based on their atomic number (the number of protons). This sets their key physical characteristics. The

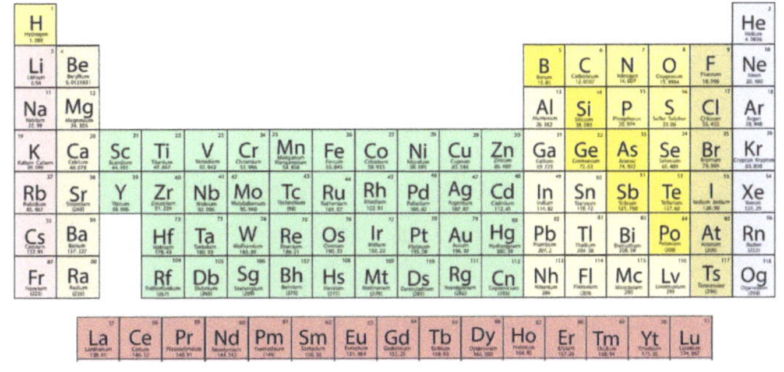

Stunning in its simplicity.

table's columns are "groups," atoms sharing the same number of electrons, which determines how they bond with other atoms—how they become stuff. The table is also color-coded by state of matter: solid, liquid, or gas. What if a business's organization chart was as clear and consistent?

Mendeleyev's organizing insight has been proven out: with no changes to its design, the Table has expanded from 63 elements in 1869 to 118 today.

What if all the elements of management—finance, human resources, operations, marketing, and so on—were as thoughtfully structured on one page? But we're getting ahead of ourselves...

Innovation sparks innovation. Ben Stein wrote in 2019 for the National Institute of Standards and Technology that "If you like engineering, the periodic table is the ultimate canvas for innovation." Marie Curie won the Nobel Prize again in 1911 for discovering polonium and radium, used for cancer therapy. It was her second Nobel.

Before turning to management, let's talk about another global standard: musical notation.

Orchestras: Musical Notation

In 1813, Beethoven composed a fifteen-minute symphony celebrating Wellington's victory at the Battle of Vittoria. It was praised as one of his best works. Arranged for an orchestra of fifty, the standard notation let his musicians perform together even though they spoke different languages, played different instruments, and hadn't heard the music before. This standard notation allows global collaborations we now take for granted.

The first form of musical notation dates from before 1400 BCE, one of the oldest systems of human thought. But the notation used by Beethoven was created in about 1000 CE by Guido of Arezzo, a Benedictine monk, to standardize and harmonize church music. More than a millennium later, the same standard system records almost all world music. It's flexible and scalable; it's written and read by street musicians as well as by the Vienna Philharmonic.

Like the periodic table, musical notation created a foundation that enables communication, collaboration, and innovation.

Next, we'll take up the central question of this book: What if managers had their own foundational system of standards?

PART II
The Standards

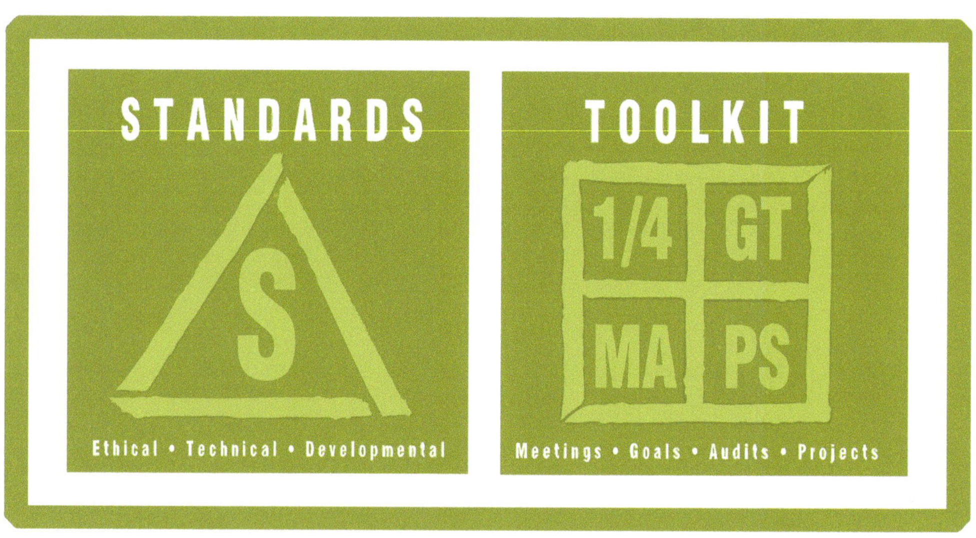

See also "The Standards Triangle" at www.theindex.net

3 · The Value of Management Standards: Morale and Margins

The World Bank reported in 2020 there were 2.7 billion people working in organizations of some kind. In other words, 2.7 billion people have a boss or are a boss. How many of them would you say are enduring faulty communications, numbing meetings, and disengaged co-workers every day?

Not well managed

The lack of ethical, technical, and developmental standards for management has been the root cause of these common and costly problems. As we'll see, standard management terms, tools, and practices now equip bosses for communicating clearly and delegating with confidence. But the benefits aren't just qualitative: using standards is profitable. A 1% improvement in management ability can boost margins by 10%.

The Case for Standards-Based Management

It's necessary to spell out the case for Standards-Based Management because some people don't believe that the terms, tools, and practices of management can be tamed and standardized. The four underlying ideas are:

1. Management is a legitimate profession with enormous financial and social value.
2. Management does not have to be chaotic; it can be sensible and straightforward.
3. Like law, engineering, and medicine, management can be learned systematically.
4. Management is a calling, a chance to help others reach their full potential.

To be clear, these standards aren't like the technical standards a plumber would use, but are standards of behavior. You're dealing with people, after all.

Management chaos is not inevitable. Without foundational standards as in chemistry and music, management is undisciplined and chaotic, and bosses get parodied in "The Office" TV shows and "Dilbert" cartoons. Lacking standards, too many people with a manager's title think the skills they need can be learned by sitting through a few workshops, videos, and a bunch of meetings. They're kidding themselves.

Delegation and Trust are the Tests of Management Strength

Margins, employee retention, customer satisfaction, and growth are the ultimate indicators of good management, but they're lagging indicators. Someone who wants to look ahead, like an experienced board member, will wonder, "Does everyone have a clear and compelling sense of direction? How do people treat each other? Is there a culture of ethical behavior, trust, and respect?" A sign of low trust and, therefore, weak delegation is a super-abundance of reporting and supervisory layers.

Board members are keenly sensitive to whether employees are genuinely engaged in the work, if they're inspired, empowered, and happy. They also watch for how well meetings are run: they look to see if the managers provide focus, facilitate honest discussion, take criticism, and are ready with reasoned and realistic alternatives. The board members can then lean back, confident the organization honors everyone's time and contributions.

But above all, board members want to see if tasks, projects, functions, and goals are crisply delegated. Managers who can't delegate aren't managers. They're bottlenecks.

Delegation occurs at two levels. The first is the hand-offs from delegators to delegates. Good managers provide clear direction and expectations, sufficient time and money,

I got it!

and just the right degree of practical and moral support. The General Management Toolkit (page 36) makes it easy to delegate a project or process.

The tools show on one page why the project or process supports the strategic plan, how it connects to everything else, what time and money are needed, and how success is evaluated. The tools are the batons in the handoff.

The General Management Index—management's technical standard (page 25)—also supports delegation at the organizational level. It provides everyone with a common language of terms and practices. That improves communication, and that leads to confident, creative, and inspired collaboration. Employees crave that kind of work and trust.

Standards + Tools = Standards-Based Management

This book will show you how to apply the three management standards using the General Management Toolkit described in Chapter 7. Standards-Based Management supports confident and effective delegation, letting you get the most from everyone's contributions.

- Ethical standard: The Pledge of Managerial Power (pages 19–20)
- Technical standard: The Index (page 24)
- Developmental standard: The Milwaukee Model (page 29)

These standards aren't rigid or static. The review board at the Center for Management Terms & Practices is responsible for evolving the input from the world community of conscientious managers.

Defining Key Terms, Including "Manager"

Everyone knows at least generally what a teacher does, what a nurse does, what a lawyer does. But if you ask ten people, "What is a manager and what do they do?" you'll get ten mumbled answers.

In Chapter 6, we'll learn the standard description of the manager's role. But in the meantime, here's clarity we can start building on:

- Management: The science and profession of running an organization
- Manager: Someone who helps people work together
- Leader: Someone who inspires others to take a risk

- Generalist: A manager who works cross-functionally, often with profit and loss responsibility
- Supervisor: A synonym for manager. Supervision is part of the manager's job.

Managers and leaders are not different people. Except for Steve Jobs of Apple, virtually no organization has a manager who isn't a leader, at least to some degree. It's flattering to be called a leader, but you can't be a leader unless you can manage. This book proves that being a good manager should be deeply respected, which starts by finally making clear just what a manager does and knows and contributes. See Chapter 6 about the Milwaukee Model. In that chapter, we elaborate on leadership ability and how it fits with the manager's job.

Why Haven't There Been Standards for Management Before?

The International Standards Organization (ISO) hosts hundreds of standards for quality and sustainability, and the American National Standards Institute (ANSI) oversees thousands of standards for safety, software, and assembly. There are standards development organizations (SDOs) protecting every sector and industry—except for general management.

If standards are so valuable, and if every industry has them, why haven't there been standards for management itself?

First, there's money in jargon. Gurus rake in billions relabeling old ideas, promising breakthroughs to make management a snap. One wonders why Harvard Business School didn't set the standards for management when it opened in 1908—but there's academic reputation in jargon, too. Though there are still breakthroughs in general management, they're rare: there's little in these standards you wouldn't find in the businesses of ancient China, Venice, or Rome.

Second, competitive managers dislike sharing ideas that give them an edge. Sharing was difficult anyway when there was no standards body to vet and recognize their contributions.

But the tallest barrier to adopting standards is fear of accountability. When managers commit to a public standard, they fear failing publicly. But it's a false fear. Like chemists, musicians, and coders, managers are much more likely to succeed when they follow sensible and accepted standards—like the musicians in Beethoven's orchestra.

Why now? The need for general management standards is pressing because markets, supply chains, and technological complexity are washing over the globe. The recent pandemic confronted even younger managers with their mortality, so now they demand meaningful work in a culture of respect. Only top-notch management ability meets today's demands of complexity and culture, both critical to recruitment and retention.

The cost of complacency. Complacency about management ability leaves cash on the table. It makes managers deaf to risks and to opportunities that develop their people. Management is challenging, but valuable and noble and, therefore, deserving of continuous and steady study.

What if There Were Simple Standards for Management?

Like chemists and musicians, standards of general management now let people pool and deploy their talents. Sharing a common "language" reduces miscommunication, the most common complaint in employee engagement surveys.

When they start with the standard best practices, managers avoid project false starts. And starting with proven practices is a natural confidence builder, which leads to innovation. An executive can see this improved idea flow in meetings that are focused, inclusive, decisive—and short. Beginning with agreement on terms slashes meeting time.

Working with standards is a gigantic step toward making each delegation of a task, project, or goal crisp and energetic. In the next chapters, we'll show how the triangle of standards is applied in a kit of simple tools for meetings, planning, process management, and project oversight.

WWW: Standardize to Globalize

The internet grew out of government projects, but it reshaped the world when global standards were established, chief among them TCP/IP (Transmission Control Protocol/Internet Protocol), FTP (File Transfer Protocol), and ICANN (Internet Corporation for Assigned Names and Numbers). Complex, but worth it.

People love achieving great things together. Great managers create every opportunity they can for people to succeed individually. They have faith that focusing on the individual guarantees the organization's success.

RECAP, ACTIVITIES, & REFLECTION

The lack of standards in general management—including definitions of management and manager—has led to costly confusion that some people now think is inevitable. Conversely, using standards makes communication and collaboration much easier.

Individual activity: Casually ask managers how they define manager and leader and how they distinguish between a manager and a supervisor. Don't press if you hear inconsistencies—let the questions sink in.

Group activity: Discuss with your fellow managers how to make delegation work well every time. See term 5.1.2.1 in The Index (www.theindex.net) for best practices.

3 Good Questions

1. What standards are essential in your industry? Why?
2. One a scale of 1 to 4, how well does delegation work in your organization?
3. How well do the manager job descriptions align with your organization chart?

Next, we start with the ethical standard because nothing matters until there's trust.

4 • The Ethical Standard: The Pledge of Managerial Power

"Power in and of itself is not bad; it only becomes so when we try to force the less powerful around us to submit to our personal will." – Thich Naht Hanh

The ethical standard of management is built on the dynamics of power: the abuse of power is the root of ethical lapses, but the wise use of power makes managers trusted and respected.

After taking time for personal reflection and thoughtful discussion, managers are encouraged to formally accept the Pledge of Managerial Power on pages 19–20. This chapter should help people understand what's at stake for the organization's performance and reputation.

People who care about others know that discussing ethics is an opportunity for personal growth.

Morals vs. Ethics

Morals are general rules for how we treat people and the planet. Some morals are proscriptive, they tell us what not to do, like the Ten Commandments: "Thou shall not..." Others are prescriptive, telling us what we should do. One of Buddhism's Precepts is, "Do good for others." The Golden Rule is the root moral. In Chapter 8, "The Promise and Rewards of Service," we'll reflect on management as a spiritual practice.

Morals are not optional. I had the misfortune to work for a man who thought it acceptable—even good—to have a high set of morals at home and none at work. Hopefully, the old-school thinking of "It's a dog-eat-dog world" will fade. The Dutch philosopher Thomas á Kempis said, "Wherever you go, there you are." You can't take a break from your moral obligations to the human race.

Ethics are applications of morals to specific situations. Most organizations, industries, and professions have codes of ethics. (See inset and The Index term 1.1.1.1 Code of ethics.) "Value Statements" are codes of prescriptive ethics that encourage people to do the right thing.

"All deceased persons shall be treated with proper care and dignity during transfer from the place of death and subsequent transportation of the remains."
— Article II-1 of the National Funeral Directors Association's Code of Professional Conduct.

The Costs of Overt and Subtle Abuses of Power

"Power tends to corrupt and absolute power corrupts absolutely." – Lord Acton

Most managers aren't aware of how much power they have over employees. Too many people are unhappy at work—even hate it—because their boss unknowingly misuses their power. A word, a glance, or a day of neglect can make an employee feel excluded, unsafe, and fearful for her or his job. The higher the level in the organization, the greater the power and the greater the effect: the chief executive can start a spiral of fear and disengagement with one public criticism or by yelling, "Just do what I tell you!" But few bosses are genuine bullies.

Most bosses unknowingly misuse their power because no one ever talked to them about it. That's why the first of the four principles of the Pledge of Managerial Power (pages 19–20) is Awareness.

My first job out of college was as a file clerk for a large real estate project in Boston. A year in, the HR manager showed up in the file room, introduced me to my new assistant, then walked away. I like to think I'm a nice guy, but I wonder if I made my helper's life a misery.

This problem is pervasive. In 2022, Gallup reported that in the United States, 50% of workers reported feeling stressed at their jobs on a daily basis, 41% as being worried, 22% as sad, and 18% as angry. The numbers are somewhat better for people working in non-profits and those with advanced education. Also in 2022, Forbes reported that, other than for reasons of pay, the top two reasons people quit their jobs are toxic company culture (62%) and poor management (56%). In other words, they don't like their bosses. Turnover is costly, particularly management turnover.

This problem spirals downward. One employee's unhappiness infects a team, frustrating the boss, who then shouts for results. That fear further inhibits people, cascading into a drop in quality, then a reduction in customer satisfaction, then fewer repeat sales, then lower margins. The organization gets a repellant reputation for a culture of mistrust and dysfunction.

How can an executive use their power to construct instead a culture of trust, appreciation, and pride? See the inset below about Paul O'Neill.

Primary Benefit of the Pledge: High Engagement

First, Do No Harm. The chief executive should make the other executives and managers aware of the risks of managerial power, and that they're expected to discuss the Pledge.

None of us are perfect. We all mistreat each other from time to time. We might have gossiped, or accidentally left someone out of a communication loop, or forgotten a promise to help. Does that mean we've behaved unethically? Yes—but only a little. It matters how we atone and if we apologize and reflect. So, we shouldn't condemn ourselves or others for being imperfect. But neither should we avoid discussing ethics because it's uncomfortable. These are the kinds of mature conversations our society needs.

> Paul O'Neill, former US Secretary of the Treasury, became CEO of Alcoa Aluminum in 1987. In his first week on the job, he used his enormous managerial power to make safety, not profits, his top priority. Wall Street predicted bankruptcy.
>
> When he retired 13 years later, Alcoa had reduced workdays lost to injury from 1.86 to 0.2 per 100 workers. Profits had quintupled.

Lead by example. The idea of power contains the power of example. No poster with a snappy quotation or a picture of people in a rowboat can counteract three seconds of an executive's misuse of power. No "soft skills" training can return 1% of the value of the chief's example. All executives should exemplify fairness and kindness every day.

Acceptance creates engagement. Some managers say, "I leave my employees alone. I just ask them to do their jobs, and I stay out of their personal lives." But this is a dereliction. Managers can't deny their employee's humanity. As we'll see in the developmental standard—The Milwaukee Model—that being a good manager absolutely depends on understanding each employee's ability, personality, potential, and aspirations. That kind of understanding is how good managers strike that fine balance between supporting and micro-managing.

I was a young property manager of a Chicago office building. A tenant had complained about the lobby's cleanliness, so the boss paid me a visit. Howard just asked me to look around the lobby. "Did you see that piece of duct tape over the entry door?" I hadn't. He smiled and left. Howard used patience, not power, to teach.

The benefits can spiral upward. If managerial ethics—the use of power—is how we treat people, it follows that the use of power largely determines what we call "people skills." The moral use of managerial power fuels productivity, loyalty, and creativity. It generates an updraft of customer satisfaction, sales, and margins. It creates a culture and reputation that are magnets for talent.

Community Ethics: Social Responsibility and Sustainability

We're connected

The LEGO Group (a family business) has a hands-on program for teaching children about social responsibility. Among the activities is building a safe haven for seahorses. It's a wonderful way to build awareness among kids that the environment is in our hands.

The collective power of a senior management team radiates far outside the organization's walls. The policies and projects of the Fortune 50 can hurt or help the economy or the environment—and set an example for the hundreds of thousands of small businesses in their supply chain (Walmart has over 100,000 vendors).

The same power dynamic applies to small organizations. The partners in a Wisconsin six-person web development business work regularly with a few soloists for design, copywriting, and social media management. While LinkedIn won't notice that one of those soloists gets dropped, it matters just as much to that gig worker as it would to Goodyear getting dropped by General Motors. Ethics don't get less important when the scale is small.

THE PLEDGE OF MANAGERIAL POWER

The Organization's Pledge

Our organization can sustain its success only when all our fellow employees are happy at work, which means they feel safe, included, and proud. We commit to the Pledge of Managerial Power because we are convinced its four principles are essential to making and keeping employees happy.

Nobody's perfect. We will occasionally make mistakes in how we use our power. However, we expect every manager to strive to treat every employee as they themselves want to be treated. Managers who misuse their power can achieve a temporary, selfish success, but we make no place in our organization for bullies or bigotry. The first principle is "do no harm."

As executives, we will set good examples and will incorporate the four principles of the Pledge in how we hire, train, support, evaluate, and reward every single employee. We all want to be respected for being fair. Our goal: strengthen our culture of trust and engaged collaboration.

The Manager's Pledge

AWARENESS Simply being aware of how their power can help or hurt will reduce mistakes and lead managers to treat their employees with fairness and kindness.

> Pledge: I will reflect often on the good and harm I can do with my managerial power.
>
> Test: When was I recently reminded of the effects of my managerial power?

– continued –

INTROSPECTION Learning to use managerial power requires introspection, which means asking questions about one's own attitudes, beliefs, and past words and actions.

> Pledge: I will be proud of learning the moral lessons of being a good manager.
>
> Test: How is being a manager making me a better person?

APPROPRIATENESS Policies provide guidelines, but every person and situation is different. Managers must listen carefully and treat each employee individually and appropriately.

> Pledge: I will think about each employee so I can manage them well in each situation.
>
> Test: How have I treated people differently in similar situations?

INTENTION It's hard to always be kind and patient, so it is important to set daily an intention to help others succeed. Learning to use one's power wisely takes maturity and strength: managers must also be kind to and patient with themselves.

> Pledge: I will use my managerial power every day to help others.
>
> Test: When did I last use my power to help an individual or group succeed?

____

Signed, Date

RECAP, ACTIVITIES, & REFLECTION

The misuse of power usually stems from managers never being made aware of how much power they have over employees. The Pledge of Managerial Power sets this important standard of behavior in a positive, constructive way.

Individual activity: Write in a confidential journal your answers to the four test questions in the Pledge. Discuss them with a mentor outside of work.

Group activity: Discussing ethics and power is sensitive. Discuss the Pledge informally with a few managers you feel already treat others with respect. Build from there.

3 Good Questions

1. When did you see a manager make a difficult, but ethical decision?
2. How does your industry or organization code of ethics make a difference?
3. When did you have to make a difficult, but ethical decision?

Ethics only matter if they're infused into every conversation and decision.

Next, we'll see how the technical standard—The Index—removes the jargon that keeps conversations from being honest, meaningful, and effective.

5 · The Technical Standard: The General Management Index

"The quality of a leader is reflected in the standards they set for themselves." – Ray Kroc

What if software developers didn't have technical standards? They'd have to reinvent their code for every app. What if plumbers didn't have standards? Pipe joints would leak, valves will blow off, and waste would back up. Like scientists using the table of elements, Ray Kroc, the founder of McDonald's, discovered he could change the world by standardizing.

The Index (next page) is the technical standard for management's terms and practices. It took five years to develop and five more to make it so easy to use. It's free at "The Index" at www.theindex.net. On your monitor or smartphone, click on any term in the hierarchy to display the context of the term (Level 1, 2, 3, or 4) and that term's definition, similar terms, three discussion questions, and vetted resources.

One plug to rule them all

Every single meeting should start with the manager asking, "Do we agree on the basic terms here?"

The Index will feel familiar. Almost all organizations have departments named after the Level 1 disciplines: Marketing and Sales, Operations, Information, Human Resources, and Finance. The "four-level, six-element" design of The Index makes it easy to remember.

The Index is about general management, not about the operational best practices unique to each industry, like how to build a building, prepare a tax return, or manufacture an appliance. The Index isn't about how to install a faucet, but how to run a plumbing company.

The Index is flexible. Like the table of elements and musical notation, The Index scales and flexes for both sole proprietors and multi-nationals. The principles of management are universal, but the opportunities for innovative application are infinite. Solid standards also give new practitioners the clarity, consistency, and confidence to succeed. We'll later explore how these standards both structure and streamline management development programs.

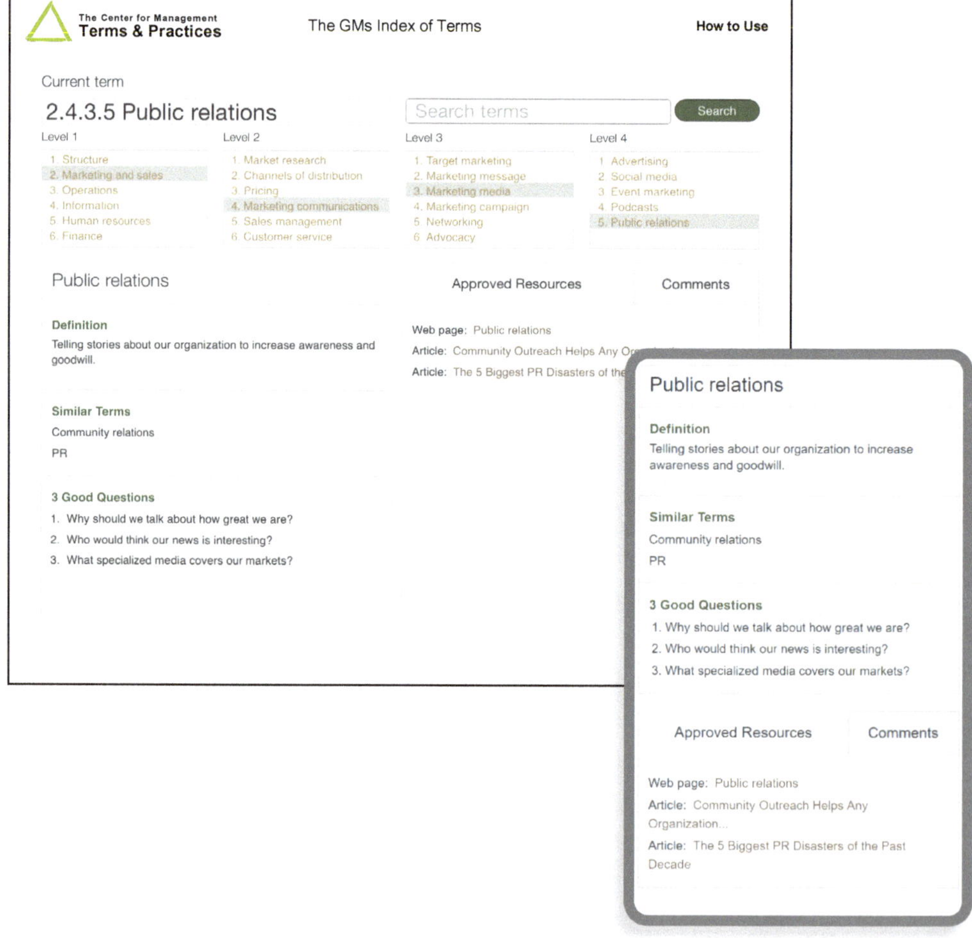

The General Management Index

See "The Index" at www.theindex.net. Click around it and watch the short "How to Use" video. Any browser will translate The Index into any language.

90% of American businesses are family owned. It's 85% in Asia and 60% in Europe. Yet, family businesses are famous for dysfunction. Agreeing on a standard language might make holiday dinners much, much easier.

Primary Benefit of The Index: Speaking the Same Language

If you gathered six experts in, say, marketing, how many would agree on what "marketing" is? Would they all know that it's "stimulating awareness, interest, trial, and commitment to your organization and its products or services" (term 2.0 in The Index). Meetings often go in circles because people aren't talking about the same thing—and don't even know it.

Like all standards, the first benefit of The Index is that it allows practitioners to understand each other, solving a common, costly, and frustrating communication problem. Managers now can start each meeting by clarifying terms.

Language and inclusion. The Index is the common language of management. It lets any manager in any department talk to the CEO in terms the CEO will understand. Speaking a standard language removes jargon as a barrier created by the elite insiders. But a common language isn't just for internal communications. I had the privilege of speaking with four Black women entrepreneurs. I asked them if the language of management was a barrier to them when speaking with bankers, accountants, investors, and other professionals. When they stopped laughing…

The Index is now free to every manager in the world. They can use it to replace miscommunication with understanding.

Primary Application: Checklist for Omissions

Besides being a standard of communications, The Index can also be used as a checklist. One way to think of The Index is as a master outline of management practices. Clicking through The Index assures both executives and managers that the work is thorough. More than once, I'd killed myself to develop a budget or plan only to have a CEO or board member lean into the table and say, "Pretty good, but did you think about X?" If necessity is the mother of invention, embarrassment is its angry aunt.

Other Applications of The Index

Aligning the organization chart to job descriptions. Few things generate more frustration, inefficiency, and ill-will than an organization chart that doesn't match the job descriptions—and that's assuming the chart and job descriptions are up to date.

One CEO pinned a poster-sized version of their organization chart in the center of the conference room wall and then pinned all the job descriptions in a constellation around it. He then put The Index up on the screen to help the executives get the chart and descriptions into alignment. It's amazing what can happen when everyone knows what they're supposed to do!

Integration in mergers and acquisitions. Harvard Business Review reported that between 70% and 90% of mergers and acquisitions fail. The costs sometimes bankrupt one of the entities. Managers of four merging NGOs spent four two-hour meetings clicking through The Index asking three questions about each management practice: Which entity has the system that the merged organization should use? Is a new system needed? and How many hours—really—will it take to create or expand that system? The board learned that it would take another year to gain the anticipated economies of scale, but they now had a realistic path. Which they then fully funded.

Assessing one's overall risk profile with the AS-IS model. Managers and planners should ask at least annually, "What could go wrong?" There are market risks, financial risks, operational risks, labor risks, cyber-security risks—in short, there are risks throughout the management spectrum. The Index is that spectrum, so it can be used to create a 360-degree risk assessment. Managers often limit their ideas of risks to what's insurable, but there are four ways to mitigate risk: Accept it, Share it, Insure it, and Shed it. It takes courage to look at all one's risks at once, but CEOs and boards hate surprises.

Preparing for a sales meeting. One good question can make all the difference in a sales meeting. Preparing good questions keeps new salespeople from making the classic mistake of launching a one-way presentation of features. The Index helps in two ways. First, its four-level structure opens lines of questioning and, second, each term already has three good open-ended questions to spark two-way discussion. In Chapter 7, you'll learn how to use the 1/4-Page Meeting Planner.

Where's our horizon?

Structuring board agendas. In Chapter 7, we'll learn how to use The Index with the Goal Tree to create a one-page strategic plan. Planning is of course the time to look over the entire horizon of issues for protecting and improving your organization. Board-run organizations, including family businesses, need an objective way to evaluate and inform board members and to make meetings focused and effective. Boards have three basic duties of oversight, vision, and goodwill. It's essential to all three that board members and advisors have a thorough if high-level understanding of the organization and how it's run.

Standards as the springboard to innovation. In 2021, blogger Erica Gage wrote, "Creativity is just combining two things that previously had nothing to do with each other and mashing them together." The periodic table of elements, as the standard language of chemistry, has prompted more valuable innovation than any other idea on earth. The Index lets managers see adjacent ideas and just begs them to find ways to work more efficiently.

The Index Integrates with The Toolkit

The General Management Index is used with all four tools in The General Management Toolkit, described in Chapter 7. The combination of standards and tools makes up Standards-Based Management.

RECAP, ACTIVITIES, & REFLECTION

The General Management Index (The Index) houses the technical standards of management, its structure, definitions, and best practices. As the common language of management, it helps solve the costly and common problems of miscommunication.

Individual activity: Use The Index to check a budget or project plan for completeness. What new ideas did you generate?

Group activity: Put The Index up at the start of the next management meeting. What do you learn just by focusing on the relevant definitions?

3 Good Questions

1. How much meeting time is lost because of misunderstanding basic terms?
2. How could The Index help in working with other organizations?
3. How might the language of management differ overseas?

How can a manager run meetings, processes, and projects if people aren't using the same terms and following the same practices?

The Index is also a framework for one's development as a manager. It can identify the things you need to learn—and things you need to teach.

But just what is the manager's job? See the next chapter.

6 · The Developmental Standard: The Milwaukee Model

"Do one thing every day that scares you. Those small things that make us uncomfortable help us build courage to do the work we do." – Eleanor Roosevelt

Trainingindustry.com found that in 2020 businesses around the world spent $358 billion on manager development. Poets & Quants reports there are 200,000 MBAs awarded annually in the United States (and MBA students collectively take on $5 billion of debt). Many employers are frustrated by people with management degrees who didn't learn how to manage people.

The #1 reason people quit is still because they don't like their boss. Something basic is missing from management education.

The Milwaukee Model of Manager Development

Innovation can occur in the way Hemingway described bankruptcy in *The Sun Also Rises:* "It happened gradually, then suddenly." The Milwaukee Model was developed after struggling for months with the question, "Where is the standard model of what a manager needs to know?" This in spite of there being 882 accredited business schools in the world, according to AACSB International in 2021.

The Milwaukee Model is the first codification of the manager's role. It answers on one page the foundational question, "What does a manager need to know?" It's foundational because until that answer is settled, it's impossible to create sensible and consistent job descriptions, design meaningful manager development programs, or build a balanced organization chart.

I. Best Practices

Refer to *The Index* for the next levels.
Generalists must be familiar with all these.

1.0 Structure
2.0 Marketing and sales
3.0 Operations
4.0 Information
5.0 Human Resources
6.0 Finance

II. Personal Development

Managing people requires maturity and a personal commitment to service.

- Handling managerial power
- Clarifying one's personal goals
- Caring for one's own health and fitness
- Improving decision-making abilities
- Developing career-long learning habits
- Cultivating peer support

III. Supervision

Managers must welcome the psychological challenges of working with people.

- Maintaining ethical behavior
- Communicating and teaching
- Assembling a team or workforce
- Leading individuals and the group
- Working through conflict
- Delegating opportunities and resources

IV. Organizational Perspective

Executives must attune their organization with market trends and external forces..

- Creating an inspiring cause and vision
- Assessing organizational risks
- Strategic planning
- Creating a culture of collaboration
- Aligning with other organizations
- Advocating in the community

The Milwaukee Model was informed by searching for commonalities among the curricula of the Ivy League business schools and by knowing it had to be communicated on a page. (Why "Milwaukee"? That's where the coffee shop was when the Model first got sketched on a napkin.)

The Model's four quadrants summarize and structure what managers must know. Appendix A is the Self-Assessment based on the Model. It includes definitions of each bulleted point.

Leader vs. Manager Clarified

On page 11, we defined "manager" as someone who helps people work together; we defined "leader" as someone who inspires people to take a risk; and we stated emphatically that these are not separate people or roles.

It's popular today to think that a leader is somehow different from and superior to a manager, that being a leader is somehow heroic and more valuable. So, in its confusion the world wastes billions and months on "leadership development" yet never gets battalions of bosses that employees admire, respect, and follow. The turning idea here: leadership ability is only part—albeit an important part—of being a good manager.

Leadership ability has three elements: audacity, eloquence, and grit. A manager, to inspire people to take a risk such as tackling a project, fulfilling a plan, or withstanding a crisis, must have the **audacity** to set a big goal. "Make no little plans!" was urban planner Daniel Burnham's instruction. Audacious goals live just inside the border of madness, barely possible yet still imaginable. They must also be important and relevant. A big goal that's untrue to the mission can ruin that organization. In practical terms, the manager must know their market and people and have confidence that the audacity of the goal will attract the ideas and investments needed to make the big leap.

Leadership ability takes more than basic communication skills. **Eloquence** is sometimes rough, sometimes smooth, sometimes erudite, often plain. Abraham Lincoln, a religious man, carried only one book with him: the collected works of William Shakespeare. If you need to energize yourself to be eloquent, copy by hand Lincoln's Gettysburg Address or Martin Luther King Jr.'s "I had a dream" speech. Or go to YouTube and listen to Greta Thunberg's speech to the United Nations, "This is all wrong." But above all, work on your writing. When asked to promote a lieutenant, Napoleon shouted, "Show me something he's written!"

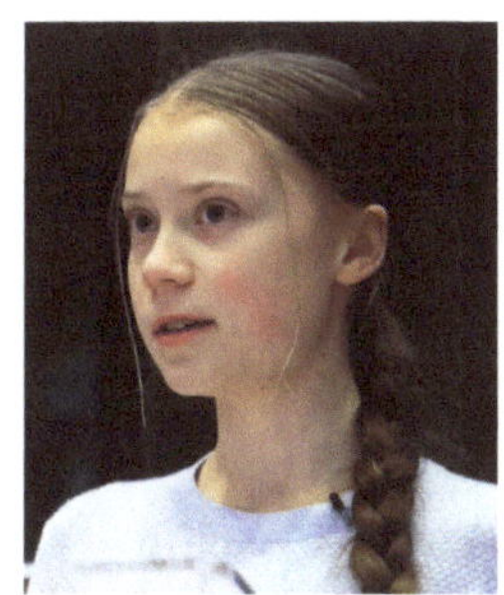
Greta got it done

Reality is a mess. Good managers know that between them and a sparkling goal are potholes, landmines, and wrong turns. There's no map to the new lands you want people to explore and conquer. Technologies will fail, people will give up, partners might betray you. The third element of leadership ability is **grit**, having the fortitude to overcome not only one's own disappointments but to buck up colleagues who stumble or beg to quit. Winston Churchill said that the first characteristic of a leader is courage because "without courage, nothing else is possible." You can develop grit by being clear that your goal is worth the suffering and that your calling as a manager is good and right.

Innovation + Management = Entrepreneurship. Innovations can be inspiring, so we often confuse innovators with leaders and managers. A great way to lose all your money is to think, "I've got recipes people love; therefore, I should run a restaurant." Inventors often start businesses with an inspiring idea but with little appreciation for the value of management—so they fail. Society needs innovators, people who sense or see a new need, but the innovators should ask themselves before they start borrowing money: Do I want to be a manager, or should I hire someone to be the manager? Studying the Milwaukee Model helps frame that relationship.

The Model's Primary Benefit: Promoting the Right People

Do no harm. Unwinding a bad management hire is incredibly costly. It's a common mistake to make someone a manager because of their superior technical ability. It can take years and cost hundreds of thousands of dollars to unwind this mistake. It will damage the organization's reputation, and worse, alienate employees. But how can you hire a good manager if no one ever standardized what a manager is supposed to know and do?

The Model is an objective basis for hiring or promoting a great manager. Hire the right manager, and the organization can jump up another level. Not only will the big metrics improve, but these managers will also build a reputation for enlightened collaboration—and that attracts other talented managers.

"Renee" struggled as a Human Resources Assistant. But her boss recognized her success in working with the other managers to implement a new HR software system. So, she was made IT Manager, where she and her team blossomed.

Create sensible job descriptions. Have you ever read a typical management job description? That's a trick question: there's been no such thing. But using the Milwaukee Model can help find and filter for the right candidate. Just as The Index is a master checklist for plans and budgets, the Model can ensure you're not missing something in your job descriptions.

Make sure they want it. The most overlooked question in a succession or development plan is, Are you *interested* in being a boss? Studying the Milwaukee Model will remind them what the job entails. They should also read the Pledge of Managerial Power so they understand that side of the job. Chapter 8 is about management as a calling: it helps candidates understand the deep rewards and personal challenges of being a boss.

If you're interviewing for a job, ask your prospective boss the bald question, "Why do you like being a man-

Standards in a Job Description

"We use the Milwaukee Model to describe and evaluate our managers. A Branch Manager needs a well-rounded set of technical Skills & Knowledge and to be above average in Personal Development and Supervision. A Branch Manager position is also a great way to begin to develop one's Organization Perspective. Candidates will be asked to complete the Model's Self-Assessment."

ager?" It's a bad sign if they say, "Hmm," and look up, hoping there's an answer on the ceiling.

Some of The Model's Other Applications

The Index as the developmental framework. In any field, students first learn its basic structure, like the table of elements, musical notation, or coding conventions. It isn't always fun, but it puts a filing cabinet in their heads so they can organize and store everything that follows. For managers, that filing cabinet is The Index.

Start with standards

The Model's Self-Assessment (see Appendix A or www.theindex.net) includes fields to enter development activities. Management can't be learned "asynchronously," which some educators say instead of "watching videos online." This might work for absorbing data, but not for learning to work with people. Development techniques for management are:

- Cross-functional projects in small groups
- Having or being a mentor
- Peer group participation
- Job rotation
- A management degree

Executives are responsible for developing their managers. They don't use people to get projects done, they use projects to develop people. They have faith that by doing so individuals and the organization will enjoy spectacular results.

Create a succession plan and management culture. Following a standard creates a convincing feeling of fairness because of its consistency and transparency. Adopting the Milwaukee Model and the Pledge of Managerial Power does just that. Executives can be effective examples only if everyone knows what standards of knowledge and behavior they're following.

A platform for innovation. Adopting standards also creates a basis for sharing ideas, which builds a strong culture. Why not have a regular internal management forum to discuss technical and interpersonal lessons? When Steve, the CEO of a paper products manufacturer, was the first to use the Model's Self-Assessment, all of the senior managers became eager to share their own ideas.

Ask for more money. Let's say you're competing for a management job. Use the Model and its assessment to make a catalog of your knowledge, skills, and attributes and (more important) how you've used them to make a provable difference to the organization.

Personality Profiles and The Model

We're all crazy. Not you, of course, but everyone else. That's the safe assumption when working with a team of people. We differ not just in skills and knowledge—what's in The Milwaukee Model—but by our personalities and how we react to people, ideas, and things.

The Milwaukee Model can be used in conjunction with personality profiles to identify and develop great managers and employees. Quadrant III of the Model is Supervision, which includes assembling a team, motivating people, and dealing with conflict.

Most systems for evaluating personalities are simplified versions of Carl Jung's theory of personality. They all have some version of Jung's scales of Extraversion-Introversion, Sensation-Intuition, Thinking-Feeling, and Judging-Perceiving. Even if no one remembers the prescriptions for dealing with different personalities, the exercise might prevent a boss from yelling, "Why can't everyone be like me?!"

Simple Ways to Learn Standards-Based Management

The easiest way is dive into Standards-Based Management is to use the 1/4-Page Meeting Planner and draft the Goal Tree, Management Self-Audit, and Projects Summary described in the next section. Just getting them started can help a lot. Don't expect perfection when learning new things. In Chapter 7 we lay out a simple way to learn, test, and implement Standards-Based Management.

Dive into the Tree

RECAP, ACTIVITIES, & REFLECTION

The Milwaukee Model of Manager Development provides a shared and simple understanding of the manager's job. It structures a consistent, complete, and sensible path to excellence and promotion, and it integrates the ethical and technical standards.

Individual activity: Work through the Self-Assessment in Appendix A or at www.theindex.net. Are you still excited about a management career?

Group activity: Discuss your Self-Assessment with your peers or boss. How can you help each other become the managers everyone wants to have?

3 Good Questions

1. Who do you know who's a manager, but not a leader—and vice versa?
2. How does your organization officially define "manager"?
3. Which of the quadrants in the Milwaukee Model interest you most?

The Pledge of Managerial Power provides a standard of ethical behavior. The Index provides a common language and body of best practices. The Milwaukee Model defines the manager's job in detail.

Next: We'll show how to apply these standards using simple tools for meetings, planning, processes, and projects.

PART III
The Toolkit

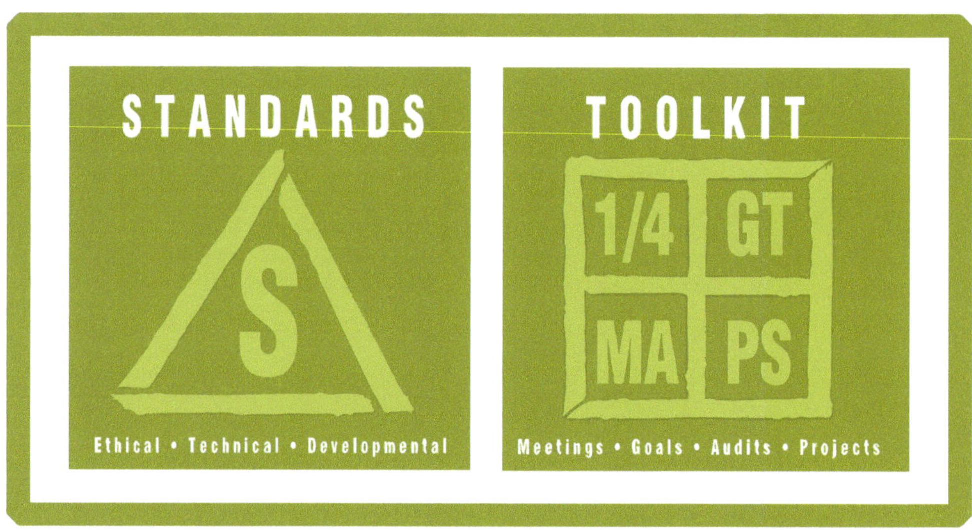

Tools at www.theindex.net/the-toolkit (no cost)

It's helpful to have printed each of the tools as well as the samples and instructions.

7 · Putting the Standards to Work

It's best to have your tools with you. If you don't, you're apt to find something you didn't expect and get discouraged." – Stephen King

Did carpenters fidget and resist when the first portable electric drill came to market in 1916? Of course. But not for long: the advantages of this new tool were so big.

New tools are scary

Drilling Into the Generalist's Four Duties

The previous chapters described the general applications of the ethical, technical, and developmental standards of management. On the next pages, we'll introduce an integrated set of tools for a manager's core duties of meeting management, planning, process management, and project oversight. These one-page tools can be downloaded at no cost at "The Toolkit" at www.index.net. You'll learn how they build on the standards and relate to one another.

The first time through feels awkward, but like the carpenters of 1916, you'll soon see how these new tools make you more productive, which makes everyone's work more profitable and rewarding.

- 1/4-Page Meeting Planner (1/4)
- Goal Tree (GT)
- Management Self-Audit (MA)
- Projects Summary (PS)

Math prodigy and physicist Blaise Pascal wrote, "I'm sorry this letter is so long. I didn't have time to write a short one." Years of refinement by hundreds of experienced managers distilled these four tools to one page each. Nobody reads page two anymore.

We're In It Together

The tools are integrated. The Projects Summary gets its direction and priorities from the Goal Tree. The Management Self-Audit identifies projects for process improvement. The 1/4-Page Meeting Planner focuses these critical discussions. And all of the tools rely on The Index to be clear and technically complete; all assume every decision meets a high ethical standard.

Placed side-by-side, the tools let everyone trace how they contribute to the plan, to productivity, and to projects that matter. A medical foundation manager said, "Now I see how what I do helps you folks!" People love to help each other succeed.

Let's open The Toolkit.

TOOL 1 of 4: 1/4-Page Meeting Planner

Abraham Lincoln said if he were to meet someone for an hour, he'd spend three hours preparing. Thanks, Abe, but who's got the time these days? The 1/4-Page Meeting Planner will quickly earn you the reputation of always asking the critical question. And asking great questions is a large part of what it means to be a great manager.

The tool can help prepare for any internal or external meeting. It can be downloaded from The Toolkit at www.theindex.net. (It's "1/4-page" because you can fold it into quarters to fit a purse or pocket.)

The Center for Management
Terms & Practices

1/4-Page Meeting Planner

Purpose

Is this meeting for ☐ a decision or ☐ information?

Leader and participants:

Date: Time:

Location:

1.0 Structure	**3.0 Operations**	**5.0 Human Resources**
Ethics and the law	Quality	Management
Competitive position	Work process	Organizational structure
Ownership structure	Production technology	Employee relations
Governance	Supply chain	Training and development
Planning	Logistics	Compensation
Facilities	Inventory	Retention and recruitment
2.0 Marketing & Sales	**4.0 Information**	**6.0 Finance**
Market research	Applications	Financial accounting
Channels of distribution	Internet	Managerial accounting
Pricing and promotions	Data and reporting	Budgeting and forecasting
Marketing communications	Research and analysis	Financing
Sales management	Communication system	Cash management
Customer service	Information technology	Risk management

3 Good Questions

Have **The GM Index** open: www.theindex.net

Term:

1

Term:

2

Term:

3

------first fold------

© 2022 CMTP, LLC

Discussion Notes

☐ Did we agree on the terms in **The GM Index**?

•
•
•
•
•
•
•
•
•
•

☐ Continued on back

The top three ★

Decisions and Tasks

1

2

3

4

5

6

☐ Did this meeting fulfill its purpose?
☐ Did we distribute and file the notes?

Exceptional Benefit: Focus Everyone's Valuable Time

Like The Index and the other three tools in Toolkit, the **1/4-Page Meeting Planner** makes sure nothing gets missed and improves communications, collaboration, and then innovation.

A meeting that's a competition isn't a meeting. If a meeting doesn't have a clear purpose, it decays into a disjointed competition to look smart. If a meeting lacks structure, people don't know how to contribute, so they just throw out ideas they hope will stick to something. Even if you've only got a few minutes to prepare for a meeting, the Planner helps you collect your thoughts quickly so you can contribute something relevant.

In this book's last chapter, which is about implementing Standards-Based Management, you'll see this "if all else fails" reminder for meetings (right).

If all else fails...

1. Define purpose and terms
2. Apply best practices
3. Ask good questions

INSTRUCTIONS: 1/4-Page Meeting Planner

It's all about the questions. Review the last meeting's notes, research the issues, and think about the people.

Steps

1. Scan The Index at www.theindex.net for three relevant terms
2. Borrow or improve on the 3 Good Questions in each term
3. Make sure the Purpose is concise and right
4. Take good notes and then record them

What if every meeting could be 15 minutes shorter?
What if you could take one meeting out of the sales cycle?

TOOL 2 of 4: Goal Tree (Plan)

"Make no little plans. They have no magic to stir men's blood and probably will not themselves be realized. Make big plans, aim high in hope and work, remembering that a noble, logical diagram once recorded will never die..." – urban planner Daniel Burnham

Planning is Difficult

Planning is consistently proven profitable, yet fewer than 10% of businesses follow a plan. Managers procrastinate because planning requires a public commitment to what they're going to do. It also lays bare what they're not going to do and what they're going to stop doing. Some goals are big, risky, and scary, so planners should take the time to absorb all the implications of everyone's aspirations, careers, and raises.

I met a CEO who kept an empty 3-inch binder on his bookshelf labeled "Strategic Plan." When people asked if he had a strategic plan, he'd just point at the binder. No one ever asked him what was in it.

The Goal Tree

Serious students of management will have heard of Silicon Valley's John Duerr's book, *Measure What Matters,* and how its OKRs (Objectives and Key Results) helped Intuit and Google launch into the stratosphere. The Goal Tree is both a plan and a dashboard to help managers at every level focus on what matters.

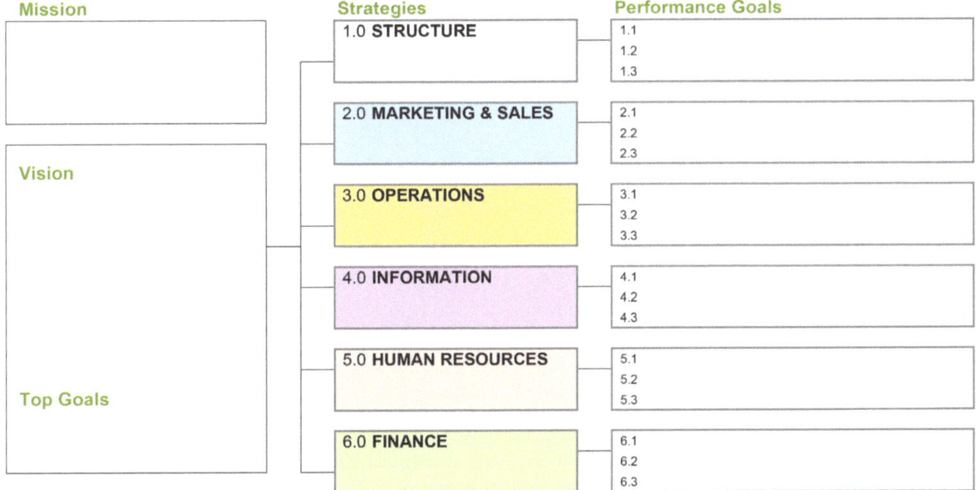

Not Your Grandfather's Strategic Plan

The Goal Tree diagrams how everyone depends on everyone through a cascading set of goals. It makes it incredibly easy to communicate your plan.

Traditional strategic planning is packed with 1950s military jargon: mission, vision, strategy, tactic, objective, and logistics. After World War II, the American military officers returned home and redeployed as corporate officers, equipped with their winning ideas and language. But it was a patriarchal, hierarchal world. But for some reason managers and consultants still cling to that language, cranking out 60-slide PowerPoints.

We'll take it from here

Exceptional Benefit: A 1-Page Delegation Map

Plans provide prioritization. Plans make people sit up a little straighter in meetings, confident they're working on the right things, helping the organization stride ahead. The form of the Tree literally maps how everyone supports the organization's purpose and goals. It's a powerful communications tool that makes priorities clear to everyone.

Not only does the Tree show how people can contribute individually; it also diagrams how they can contribute collectively. Remember our definition of a manager? **Someone who helps people work together.** The Tree shows everyone why they're a team and why it's so valuable to have managers who can work cross-functionally.

The Tree is also a map of delegation and promotion. Reading it from right to left, it is an illustration of ever-increasing span of responsibility and challenge. It should also help people appreciate just how complex the executive's job is.

A word about a word. Lots of people are befuddled by the word "strategy." That's because it's a perfect synonym for "plan:" a "strategic plan" means "a plan-like plan." Isn't a strategic plan supposed to improve clarity?

So, instead of saying "strategy," say either "overall plan" or "general approach" as in "What's our overall plan?" or "What's our general approach to marketing this year?" Get a reputation for clear speaking.

A note for very large businesses. I was helping a multinational plan a 1,000,000-square-foot facility renovation for five global business units. A goal was of course to share resources as much as possible. But none of the units had a strategic plan; all they had was incomplete notes and slide decks. So, we abstracted those as best we could into five Goal Trees, using standard terminology from The Index. When we put those five one-page Trees next to each other in front of the executives, they erupted with a stream of questions: Why are we using different metrics? How come only two units have a client retention goal? Why didn't the goals align with the corporate strategic plan? It was a powerful, helpful conversation that substantially improved ROI on the capital project by creating meaningful collaborations.

For testing Standards-Based Management, start with a team of senior managers. If you already have a plan, start by abstracting it into the Tree. If you don't have a plan, brainstorm two or three critical measurements for each department. Have The Index up on a screen to keep from missing a key management practice.

But first, let's define the simple-sounding word "goal."

The four levels of management goals. All management goals describe a change for the better. To say "My goal is to install the new software" isn't describing a change of condition, it's stating the obvious about a project. What's important isn't installing the software; it's how the software is supposed to change things.

Management goals have four levels of precision, and the Goal Tree combines them in a meaningful context. The most precise are the **performance goals** for each management discipline. These goals have two numbers and a date, such as "Improve board self-evaluation score from 4.2 to 4.7 by December 202X" (some people call these SMART goals). The next level are the **top goals** for the entire organization, seen in the lower left of the Tree. It takes nice judgment to pick these three, but they should be relevant and inspiring to every department. They should in some way relate to the "iron triangle" of speed, cost, and quality.

The next two types of goals aren't measurable. The **vision** statement is a qualitative goal describing the deep desires the organization has for itself, but it's still a goal, a change of condition. The **mission** statement is a goal, too: it captures how the organization should make the world a better place.

INSTRUCTIONS: Goal Tree

Estimated time for first draft: Three two-hour meetings
Relevant definitions and practices from The Index:

- 1.5.1 Business planning
- 1.2 Market position
- 4.4 Research and analytics

While you can start using the Goal Tree with any of the four goal types, this sequence is usually easiest:

1. Fill in **Performance Goals** for each discipline
2. Brainstorm three words to characterize each discipline (colored boxes)
3. Draft the **Top Goals** for growth, efficiency, and quality
4. Distill a **Vision** from a brainstorm of three long-term changes in each discipline
5. Create a **Mission** by answering, "How do we make the world a better place?"
6. Review the Tree monthly, using use the progress columns on the right

The Goal Tree is the sheet music for your organization's next performance.

TOOL 3 of 4: Management Self-Audit

"There are... two kinds of people: those who are changing and those who are setting themselves up to be victims of change." – Jim Clemmer

How to Add 1% to Gross Margin Just By Thinking

One new idea or technology can make a process or practice obsolete overnight. Processes and practices link, so updating one can force updates to many. A diligent review of core workflows is obviously important when your world's been shaken up by a growth spurt, recession, sale, or merger. The Management Self-Audit's rows are keyed to The Index, so it ensures all processes get examined. It's a valuable team discussion.

It's a **self**-audit because no outsider really knows how things work and having an outsider in the room gets you rose-colored answers. Left to themselves, managers dig deeper. It's human nature to remember what's broken and forget what worked, but it's inspiring to build on strengths. You just have to agree on what those strengths are.

Don't fall behind

The Management Self-Audit

X Not critical this year
E **E**xcellent
A **A**dequate
N **N**eeds attention

		Last year	This year	Response
1	**STRUCTURE**			
1.1	Ethics and the law	A	N	Apply for patent on Widget Z
1.2	Market position	A	A	Need to study market for coming gaps
1.3	Ownership structure	X	A	Reconsider after market studies
2	**MARKETING & SALES**			
2.1	Market research	N	A	Use Competitor's Grid from The Center
2.2	Channels of distribution	N	A	Strengthen new dealer relationships
2.3	Pricing	A	N	Run 80/20 analysis to spot targets
3	**OPERATIONS**			
3.1	Quality	E	A	Study product life cycle
3.2	Work process	N	N	Study value of specialized facilities
3.3	Production technology	A	N	Improved assembly velocity 20%
4	**INFORMATION**			
4.1	Applications	A	N	Prepare for ERP upgrade in 24-30 months
4.2	Internet	A	N	Update for next year
4.3	Data and reporting	E	E	No significant changes needed
5	**HUMAN RESOURCES**			
5.1	Management	A	N	Continue in Center Workgroups
5.2	Organizational Design	A	N	New maps to affect job descrips
5.3	Employee Relations	A	N	Policies need update
6	**FINANCE**			
6.1	Financial accounting	A	A	New software working well
6.2	Managerial accounting	N	A	Incorporate into staff orientation
6.3	Budgeting and forecasting	A	A	No major projects foreseen

Exceptional Benefit: Optimize to Maximize Margins

Optimizing processes and keeping them that way. It's an egotistical team that thinks it can't improve, but it's costly to fix processes only after they've broken. The Audit lets far-sighted managers work efficiently to improve efficiency, first by helping cull outdated processes and then by spotlighting improvement opportunities. The first year's top-to-bottom process review will naturally take more time than the next year's.

Like the Goal Tree, distilling issues to a page takes courage. You need to confront what's not been working and what's been overlooked. The executives should take fear of blame off the table by clearly taking responsibility for everything.

Create a "stop" plan. A breakthrough in workflow analysis (see The Index, term 3.2.1) is when a process can be eliminated or merged. So, your first question might be, "What can we stop doing?" No one wants to waste their time. It feels great to work efficiently—and it validates our pay.

Knowledge management vs. management turnover. The more management processes you optimize and record, the less the loss when a manager retires, quits, or

INSTRUCTIONS: Management Self-Audit

Estimated time for first draft: Three to four 2-hour meetings
Relevant definitions and practices from The Index:

- 3.2 Work process
- 5.3.4 Employee policy
- 4.1 Applications

Open the Self-Audit and The Index on a large screen or two. Participants should prepare by clicking through The Index for best practices of concern. The discussion questions and the Approved Resources in The Index will help managers explore these processes and practices deeply.

Steps

1. Assign a scribe. Enter "X" for irrelevant practices. Don't overthink the ratings
2. Agree on the few high-priority processes or systems to work on
3. Follow up on opportunities for cross-functional collaboration
4. Run the Self-Audit every year

moves into a different unit or role. It's common for the Self-Audit conversation to lead to cross-training—and learning how to record workflows. These discussions are rich team-building exercises, so accept that the conversation will jump from department to department.

People love to work efficiently. The Audit makes them feel their work really matters.

The Triangle of Optimization

The triangle icon above reminds managers to search constantly for opportunities to improve **speed, cost**, and **quality** in everything.

In the short run, managers can improve speed, cost, or quality only at the expense of the others. "Yes, we can meet your deadline, but we'll either have to charge more or build to a lesser spec." Or "Yes, we can add those features at the original cost, but it'll take another week."

But in the long run, managers can improve all three. Sometimes innovation comes in a blast (barcode scanning), but often it's like Edison's light bulb: patiently testing 6,000 filaments. The Self-Audit, informed by the terms and best practices in The Index, brings a system to optimization.

Breakthroughs in efficiency can create spectacular competitive advantages. And making the best use of people's time makes them feel good about their work.

TOOL 4 of 4: Projects Summary

You're Doing Much Too Much

Most managers over-commit to projects because they never see all the hours they've promised. The Projects Summary snaps time, cost, urgency, and importance into focus. As a report, it reassures executives and boards that managers have their priorities clear, and that people are working to—but not beyond—capacity.

The Projects Summary

	Priority	Status	PM	$K	Hrs	Goal	Comments	YEAR 1 1QTR	2QTR	3QTR	4QTR
STRUCTURE											
Create campus master plan	H		LM	30	200	1.1	Facilities, phasing and dock flow				
Run board self-evaluation	M		DT	0	24	1.3	See The Index 1.4.1 Board of Directors				
MARKETING & SALES											
Update logo	L		BD	9	80	2.1	Using B&W Advertising				
Complete competitor research	H		KL	12	24	2.5	Telephone interviews				
OPERATIONS											
Change steel vendors	M		BR	20	80	3.1	Consider future tariff issues				
Upgrade packaging machine	M		LM	25	120	3.3	Before assembly line rework				
INFORMATION											
Update ERP module X	H		AA	30	80	4.1	Update workflow diagrams essential				
Install business intelligence software	M		KL	36	100	4.2	Consolidate management reports				
HUMAN RESOURCES											
Update HRIS	M		DR	22	120	5.1	Need to add training hours				
Update employee engagement survey	H		DR	0	40	5.2	See 5.3.2 Best Practices				
FINANCE											
Run Cost/Benefit Worksheet on Equipment X	H		HM	0	12	6.2	Will need detailed income projections				
Renegotiate Letter of Credit	H		HM	5	40	6.1	Work with attorney				

Exceptional Benefit: Cut Project Meetings in Half

Projects, including those brought to the surface by the Goal Tree and Management Self-Audit, transform organizations and make careers. But they can be career risks if they fail. So, use this proven tool to avoid false starts and flops.

The executives of a large manufacturer finally totaled all the hours for their projects. They found that each had committed all 2,000 working hours in the year, leaving no time for their daily duties. The CEO laid down the law: **managers could only work on three projects at a time.** People could then feel proud of what they'd accomplished, and more got done.

Review meetings don't have to be endless problem-solving brainstorms. Be strict in review meetings: discuss first those projects with problems (red) and then those at risk (yellow). But don't try to solve every problem there. The meeting leader will develop a sense for ending large group discussions and scheduling smaller, separate sessions to get projects back on their rails.

There's no need to take the whole team's time discussing projects that are on track (green) but do take a moment to recognize teammates for their contributions.

INSTRUCTIONS: Projects Summary

Estimated time for first draft: Four 2-hour meetings
Relevant definitions and practices from The Index:

- 5.1.4 Project management
- 4.1.5 Collaboration software
- 5.3.6 Performance evaluation

Enter all big projects already underway, then add projects to fulfill the goals in the Goal Tree. Drill into how many participants are in how many project meetings and the actual time for individual tasks—then add 25% more hours as a contingency. Doing new things means you don't know everything.

Steps

1. Enter short project titles and comments
2. Assign one project manager
3. Link to the relevant strategic goals in the Goal Tree to make priorities plain
4. Fill in the quarterly Gantt Chart (timeline) last. Revise the sequence as needed
5. Draft a separate detailed timeline for very large projects

The Projects Summary lets everyone see how their work on projects matters to the organization. Using the four tools together lets everyone see how their decisions matter.

Next, we explore what it means to take up management as a calling, as a career of service.

PART IV
Management As A Calling

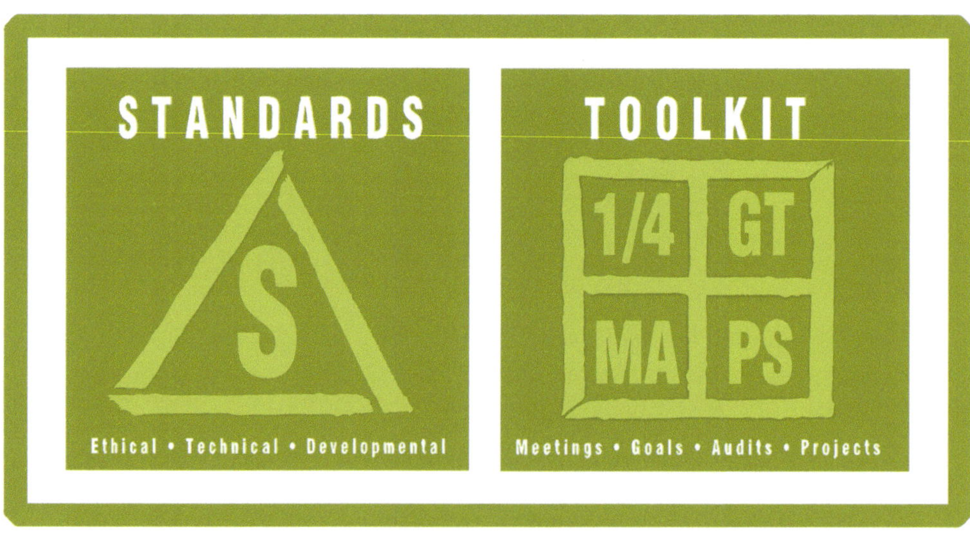

8 · Finding Meaning and Rewards in Service

"It was in my heart to help a little for I had been helped much." – Khalil Gibran

Managers are mentors and teachers. In 2000, five hundred former students attended the memorial service for Greg Baker, a Chicago high school English teacher and swim coach. One student, William Horberg, now chair emeritus of the Producers Guild of America, said, **"If we are lucky, we all have had that teacher or mentor who touched our core and gave us inspiration or direction or a good old-fashioned kick in the butt..."**

Mentors are forceful

Some people seek management titles for the immediate rewards of pay, power, and status. But dedicated managers treasure the lasting rewards of the successes and happiness of others. This takes exceptional competence and maturity—but having five hundred people at your memorial proves your career was well spent.

Making Work Meaningful: Reminders About Social Value

Humans are social beings, so they crave work that's valuable to society. Happiness isn't material gain, perfection, or comfort: employees are made happy with meaningful work and competent, caring bosses. Sadly, a lot of people no longer believe they can be happy at work. Let's turn that around.

Remind them of the good they already do. It's human nature to dwell on problems instead of achievements. Even police officers lose track of how they help. So, a manager's first challenge isn't usually to create meaning but to remind people of it. One vivid story about how your product or service changed a customer's life will inspire your organization for years.

Everyone counts. Firefighters provide obvious social value, but a new accounts payable clerk might lose sight of how they contribute to their organization's financial health. Many of us support people who support other people, and few of us need to be heroes. But we all need to know in at least some small way that our work matters.

The COO of a Chicago-based manufacturer of springs was asked if it was disappointing that their products disappeared into the guts of cars, medical devices, and appliances. He answered with a piece of industrial poetry about being a small cog: **"Our springs bring equipment to life."**

Work doesn't have to be unique to be meaningful. Differentiation makes us feel special, but it adds zero to meaning. A Wisconsin hospital blew $300,000 having a mission statement written. Don't we all know what a hospital does and that it's important? You don't have to be chief neurosurgeon to be proud of how you help: each of America's four million nurses can feel that same pride.

Jargon is a barrier to meaning. The greatest value of The Index is that it breaks the insidious barriers of management jargon. And the jargon about meaning at work is particularly perilous: Mission, Vision, Purpose, Values, "The Why." Don't have more than one document about meaning. Use video and images to show why your work together makes the world a better place.

To Err is Human

Like other callings—as coach, counselor, teacher—a manager must hold mature and realistic expectations of their fellow humans. You can't develop people unless you let them try new things, and trying new things means they'll make mistakes. Good managers' plans provide leeway for experimentation and learning.

There's a story about Tom Watson, the CEO of IBM who transformed it into a global powerhouse. A manager had made a $10 million error and thought when he was called into Watson's office that he was going to be fired. Watson said, **"Fire you? I just spent $10 million educating you!"**

E Pluribus Unum ("Out of the many, one"). Section III of the Milwaukee Model (page 30) is "Supervision." Good managers don't just work with individuals, but with duos, trios, and quartets. Team-building also takes experimentation and forgiveness. Managers know patience and forgiveness pay off in loyalty and innovation. The whole is greater than the sum of the parts. That's why we create companies in the first place.

The Key Personal Characteristic is Maturity

"Maturity begins when one lives for others." – Hermann Hesse

The Model makes plain that most of management is about working with people, what's often called "supervisory ability." Working with people takes maturity, which includes two things: the emotional strength to deal calmly with co-workers' quirks and the wisdom to see into the practical reality of a charged situation.

The three other characteristics of mature managers. Managers need the **courage** to make decisions that entail risk and disappointments. They need the **curiosity** to keep exploring new ideas and opportunities for everyone. And they need the **compassion** to make kindness their first impulse, even when they themselves have been mistreated.

"Leadership development" is often a euphemism for trying to make people more mature. But like any comforting jargon, it softens the seriousness of the issue, which means the issue never gets resolved.

The Rewards Are Great but Subtle

"A leader is best when people barely know he exists…they will say, 'we did it ourselves'."
– Lao Tzu

The three rungs of a manager's career ladder are progressively abstract, responsible, and lonely:

1. Manager
2. Executive (a manager of managers)
3. Chief executive

Indirect personal rewards. While an increased span of authority allows you to accomplish more, it's important to be emotionally prepared for increasingly subtle rewards. Switching from specialist to manager instantly switches your reward system from getting recognition for a tangible, technical accomplishment to basking in the indirect glow of your team's success. It's another shift when making the step to an executive job, when you're a manager of managers. You must learn to "fly by the instruments," seeing progress through second-hand reports and opinions.

And the chief executive's job is yet again vastly different and more subtle. After being promoted from CFO where he'd worked for thirty years, one CEO said, "Two days later, no one asked me out to lunch anymore." It was lonely, but a year later he felt in his bones how he'd helped the entire organization grow and stabilize.

Developing Oneself as a Manager with a Calling

"The eyes see everything but themselves." — Yugoslavian proverb

Learning the technical standards of general management is straightforward (see The Index and Chapter 5), but developing emotional maturity and wisdom is subtle. Our egos blind us to mistaken ideas about ourselves and our relationships, so managers must be able to look inward with courage.

I see me

Take the Pledge of Managerial Power (Chapter 4). But it's not enough to read it, sign it, and shelve it. It takes constant study. You might rewrite your answers to the Pledge's four test questions each quarter:

1. When was I recently reminded of the effects of my managerial power?
2. How is being a manager making me a better person?
3. How have I treated people differently in similar situations?
4. When did I last use my power to help an individual or group?

Journalling is also helpful for developing your calling. In *How to Win Friends and Influence People,* Dale Carnegie wrote about himself that

> "For years I kept an engagement book showing all the appointments I had during the day. My family never made any plans for me on Saturday night, for the family knew that I devoted a part of each Saturday evening to the illuminating process of self-examination and review and appraisal. After dinner, I went off by myself, opened my engagement book, and thought over all the interviews, discussions, and meetings that had taken place during the week. I asked myself: What mistakes did I make that time? What did I do that was right – and in what way could I have improved my performance? What lessons can I learn from that experience? ... This system of self-analysis and self-education continued year after year, [and] did more for me than any other one thing I have ever attempted."

You owe your staff careful thought. Perhaps in the same journal (kept locked up at home), you could write and update profiles of the people you manage. What are their skills? What are their interests both at and outside of work? Are they introverts or extraverts? Having used a personality profile system can help. You might discover you'd underestimated someone's potential because you hadn't thought hard enough about them. You might also come to realize that one of your staff just isn't suited to their job or ready for a promotion.

Don't manage alone. Working with people is a subjective, emotional, and limitless study. Having a mentor as well as a small and trusted peer group is so important to developing yourself and as a check against impulsive decisions.

Read the right management books. Many management books focus on quick fixes, so for deeper understanding, try the books in Appendix C. Book discussion groups can help expand and challenge your thinking.

Great art and the mystery of being human. Great art opens deep insights into human nature. Charles Dicken's *Pickwick Papers* has 356 characters. But if you don't have time for Dickens or for *War and Peace* (written the same year Mendeleyev recorded the table of elements), try any other of the 10,000 classics. Don't waste your life reading junk.

People are mysterious

A Sensitive Subject: Management as Spiritual Practice

"My religion is kindness." – The Dalai Lama

Not everyone is comfortable linking their work with their spiritual or religious life. It's unethical to use one's managerial power to pressure anyone—even gently—to believe as you do. It's a conversation to have only with yourself or your spiritual teacher.

But for many people and many cultures, work and faith are intrinsically linked. Christianity, Islam, Buddhism, Hinduism, and Judaism are rich with scripture about work and working with others. All the world's religions command us to practice kindness, patience, and humility. They all call us to promote the common good by obeying the Golden Rule, to "Treat others the same way you want them to treat you." It's up to the reader to reflect on how being a manager—having power—can be a spiritual test and teaching.

Delegation is also a test of faith. Delegation takes faith in the potential goodness of others. It requires humility: the willingness to admit others are sometimes better. It also takes patience and forgiveness when employees make mistakes, as we all do. And it requires the wisdom to see a sunlit horizon beyond today's inevitable struggles and stumbles.

Everyone's Included

What if every manager in the world used the same terminology? What if they used the same tools and studied the same best practices? And what if you and they were part of a global community helping people on opposite sides of social, cultural, and political borders?

RECAP, ACTIVITIES, & REFLECTION

People still get promoted into management roles because of their technical abilities—always with bad results. A management career is an opportunity to serve others and to develop personally. The challenges and rewards are subtle, but profound.

Individual application: Great managers, like teachers and nurses, are both competent and compassionate. How does being a manager reflect your deepest values?

Group activity: Discuss your organization's criteria for hiring and promoting managers. What makes employees loyal to their bosses? Not everyone is called to management.

3 Good Questions

1. Think of your favorite manager. How many people did they help?
2. When did your core product or service change someone's life?
3. When did a management challenge make you a better person?

By taking up management as a calling, you can be proud of and respected for having helped so many people achieve so much together.

In our next and last chapter, you'll see simple ways to try Standards-Based Management in your work and in your organization.

PART V
Trial & Implementation

STANDARDS-BASED MANAGEMENT

9 · Applying Standards-Based Management

This book set out to prove that, like chemistry and music, management needs standards to be taken seriously and to create value for individuals, organizations, and society.

Applying the standards of the Pledge of Managerial Power, The Index, and the Milwaukee Model is the antidote to fragmented, frustrating, and unprofitable work. Standards-Based Management is a framework that can yield practical and spectacular results for any size or type of organization. It's also the roadmap for a management career journey.

Why Change?

Communication improves when everyone uses the same terms, tools, and practices. When communication improves, people become more excited about working together and they get better and better results. Those successes strengthen their faith in the standards and that frees the boss from "people issues" so they can seek out big new opportunities for everyone.

A skeptic might say, **"We're pretty successful, so why change? It's scary."** You and your teammates work hard, provide high-quality products and services, and truly care about each other and your customers. These are wonderful. But if it's good to be successful, it's better to be more successful: more collaborative, more innovative, more efficient, more trusted.

Can Standards-Based Management Improve Delegation in Your Organization?

In Chapter 1 we asserted that delegation was the proof of management ability. Individual managers need to be able to delegate well, and the organization needs to support those handoffs with the right culture and resources. Without delegation, the organization isn't taking full advantage of its human capital, it's limited by the time and ability of the top people. We form into groups to leverage our collective talents and interests, after all.

Are there any other management indicators you'd like to change? Check those you'd like to work on first. Experienced managers understand focusing on one will improve the others.

- ☐ Clear communication
- ☐ A trusting and collaborative culture
- ☐ A steady pace of innovation
- ☐ High employee engagement
- ☐ Steady manager development
- ☐ Sensible organization design
- ☐ Process efficiency
- ☐ Strong project performance
- ☐ Clear prioritization
- ☐ Strategic planning

Simple Steps

1. Use The Index as a checklist for a budget or project plan (Chapter 5)
2. Try the 1/4-Page Meeting Planner to make meetings meaningful (Chapter 7)
3. Discuss The Pledge (Chapter 4)

Piloting

Form a team of experienced managers from each department to draft the four tools in the Toolkit, using the instructions in Chapter 7.

TOOLKIT
1/4 GT
MA PS
Meetings • Goals • Audits • Projects

The first time through might generate some friction and frustration—but persevere. Remember how often you yearned to have everyone on the same page. the Index, the Pledge of Managerial Power, the Milwaukee Model, and The Toolkit are those pages.

If the pilot succeeds, an executive could use the text below to announce the adoption of Standards-Based Management.

Email re: Adopting Standards-Based Management

Miscommunication is the Big Barrier to Collaboration, Innovation, and Inclusion

We all love working together on something bigger than ourselves. That passion is the most powerful and positive motivation in management. Together, we can do anything. Together, we can realize our full potential as individuals and as an organization.

But miscommunication often gets in our way. If we can't communicate, we can't collaborate, and if we can't collaborate, we can't innovate. Getting the big things done takes everyone working and thinking together. That's why we're adopting **Standards-Based Management** and its ethical, technical, and developmental standards: the **Pledge of Managerial Power, The General Management Index,** and **The Milwaukee Model of Manager Development.** Standards-Based Management builds inclusion by giving us a common language.

As the senior manager, I have primary responsibility for clear communications throughout our organization.

Even changes for the better can be frightening. But the senior managers have piloted Standards-Based Management and are confident everyone will find it sensible, easy, and rewarding. We'll soon share the four tools from **The General Management Toolkit:** the 1/4-Page Meeting Planner, Goal Tree, Management Self-Audit, and Projects Summary.

Meetings with Meaning

Meetings reveal how well we communicate, collaborate, and innovate. So, from now on, all meetings will have a short agenda. Its format is up to the meeting leader, but it will include a one-sentence statement of purpose, a list of the few most relevant terms and practices (see The Index), and concise notes. Everyone should bring three good questions to every meeting.

– continued –

Training and Resources

The Center for Management Terms & Practices (www.theindex.net) is the standards body for general management. Its publication, *Atoms & Orchestras: The Case for Standards-Based Management,* describes this simple, scalable system in detail. Next week, we'll provide the schedule for how we'll roll out Standards-Based Management, answer your questions, and begin providing training and support.

The Three Habits

If you ever find following the standards confusing, just remember these three key habits: 1) Define purpose and terms, 2) Follow best practices, and 3) Ask good questions.

Management ability is our #1 competitive advantage. It lets all of us deploy and develop our talents to our maximum potential. The more we collaborate, the more we'll accomplish!

If All Else Fails, Remember These Three Things

A friend of mine was given what he thought was a plum assignment early in his career at a large manufacturer. He was asked to run the "Reconfiguration Committee." But after three long meetings with twenty people, Bruce confessed he didn't know what "reconfiguration" really meant. After an awkward silence, everyone else admitted they didn't know either. It had something to do with standardizing production processes, but no one was quite sure…

If all else fails...

1. Define purpose and terms
2. Apply best practices
3. Ask good questions

Meetings are the mirror of management ability. They showcase the manager's ability to communicate clearly, foster collaboration, and delegate crisply. Everyone wants meetings to be positive, productive, and even fun.

Yes, learning and practicing Standards-Based Management takes time and effort. But it will let you feel the intense pride of helping people achieve great things together!

Contact the Center for Management Terms & Practices at www.theindex.net to learn about training and certification in Standards-Based Management.

APPENDICES

Appendix A: Milwaukee Model Self-Assessment

See Chapter 6 about The Milwaukee Model of Manager Development as the Developmental standard. You can also download the Model and Self-Assessment from www.theindex.net.

I. Best Practices

Refer to *The Index* for the next levels. Generalists must be familiar with all these.

1.0 Structure
2.0 Marketing and sales
3.0 Operations
4.0 Information
5.0 Human Resources
6.0 Finance

II. Personal Development

Managing people requires maturity and a personal commitment to service.

- Handling managerial power
- Clarifying one's personal goals
- Caring for one's own health and fitness
- Improving decision-making abilities
- Developing career-long learning habits
- Cultivating peer support

III. Supervision

Managers must welcome the psychological challenges of working with people.

- Maintaining ethical behavior
- Communicating and teaching
- Assembling a team or workforce
- Leading individuals and the group
- Working through conflict
- Delegating opportunities and resources

IV. Organizational Perspective

Executives must attune their organization with market trends and external forces..

- Creating an inspiring cause and vision
- Assessing organizational risks
- Strategic planning
- Creating a culture of collaboration
- Aligning with other organizations
- Advocating in the community

Manager	
Supervisor	
Date	

Instructions

1. Manager and their boss discuss the Model
2. Manager assesses themself
3. Manager and boss discuss the assessment and agree on what to learn that year
4. They choose development activities and active projects
5. They evaluate progress and adjust as needed
6. Toward the end of the year, they re-evaluate the manager's performance

I. Best Practices

The standard body of knowledge for general management practices. For practical decision-making, applying general principles and industry knowledge.

Open The GM Index at www.theindex.net. Click through levels 1, 2, and 3 for definitions and context. Use the Management Self-Audit tool in The GM Toolkit if helpful.

Self-rating scale: 1 to 4.
1=Area of focus.
4=Mastery in current role.
X=Not yet relevant.

Note: Rate yourself in the context of your position and organization. Don't rate yourself lower because you're not the CEO of General Motors.

	Self-rating
1.0 Structure	________
2.0 Marketing and sales	________
3.0 Operations	________
4.0 Information	________
5.0 Human resources	________
6.0 Finance	________

Top 3 things to work on this year (development activity)	% complete
1.	
2.	
3.	

II. Personal Development

Managing people requires maturity and a personal commitment to service.

Self-rating scale: 1 to 4: 1=Area of focus. 4=Mastery for current role.
X=Not relevant. See samples of tools at The GM Toolkit.

Self-rating

Handling managerial power ________

Knowing how to monitor and improve how you use managerial power in different situations. Read the Pledge of Managerial Power to learn how much your power staff can help and hurt them.

Clarifying one's personal goals ________

Knowing what you want to be and achieve and who you want to be as a person. Thinking objectively about the sources of your beliefs and attitudes. Being confident you can put other people first.

Caring for one's own health and fitness ________

Understanding the level of physical and mental fitness needed to be an attentive and engaged manager. Setting a positive example of sound habits and sensible self-discipline. Avoiding burnout.

Improving decision-making abilities ________

Using different kinds of quantitative and qualitative information to help your staff create good solutions. Being aware of your own conscious and subconscious processes for making different kinds of decisions.

Developing career-long learning habits ________

Accepting that even successful chief executives always have things to learn. Having learning goals, healthy personal interests, and channels for finding facts. Seeking challenging perspectives.

Cultivating peer support ________

Actively and regularly seeking peers for information, ideas, challenges, and moral support. Purposely seeking new acquaintances who will challenge your ideas as well as your attitudes and beliefs.

Top 3 things to work on this year (development activity)	% complete
1.	
2.	
3.	

III. Supervision

Managers must welcome the moral, ethical, and psychological challenges of working with people.

Self-rating scale: 1 to 4: 1=Area of focus. 4=Mastery for current role. X=Not relevant. For background, refer to relevant terms and Approved Resources in The GM Index.

Self-rating

Maintaining ethical behavior ________
Defining morals and ethics. Understanding the letter and spirit of your Code of Ethics. Anticipating ethical dilemmas and leading those discussions. Responding to unethical or possibly unethical behavior.

Communicating and teaching ________
Listening with comprehension, sympathy, and objectivity. Sharing ideas in writing, speaking, and through images. Inspiring people by making the big goals vivid and exciting.

Assembling a team or workforce (tool: Management Self-Audit) ________
Knowing the mix of skills, experiences, time, and support for a project or process. Creating the right balance of perspectives and personalities. Knowing when to remove someone or disband the group.

Leading individuals and groups ________
Knowing each of your staff well enough to stimulate their particular talents and energy. Having the audacity, eloquence, and grit to lead, inspire people to take a risk, and overcome obstacles.

Working with conflict ________
Having the maturity, patience, and skill to direct each staff member. Having the firmness and skills to resolve conflicts promptly and constructively. Eliminating barriers among departments.

Delegating opportunities and resources (tool: Projects Summary) ________
Understanding the staff's workload and personal and collective capacity. Creating assignments that are challenging, but not overwhelming. Managing with minimum intervention.

Top 3 things to work on this year (development activity)	% complete
1.	
2.	
3.	

IV. Organization Perspective

Executives must attune their organization to market trends and external forces.

Self-rating scale: 1 to 4: 1=Area of focus. 4=Mastery for current role. X=Not relevant. For background, refer to relevant terms and Approved Resources in The GM Index.

Self-rating

Creating an inspiring cause and vision ________
Understanding if a challenge will matter deeply to every employee. Expressing the facts and feelings of that challenge so everyone will eagerly take on the risks and discomforts of change.

Assessing organizational risks ________
Having the information to know what could go wrong in each management discipline (The Index). Knowing if the organization can add risks or isn't risking enough.

Strategic planning (tool: Goal Tree) ________
Creating a challenging, yet realistic and balanced mix of short- and long-term goals to advance the organization's cause and vision. Keeping the organization focused on the goals.

Creating a culture of collaboration (tool: 1/4-Page Meeting Planner) ________
Understanding how all the formal and informal rules of behavior help everyone contribute the most, individually and collectively. Knowing when and how to reshape those rules.

Aligning with other organizations ________
Working to the mutual benefit of new and existing customers, vendors, and affiliates. Anticipating and then adjusting to changes to any part of that overall network.

Advocating in the community ________
Working with industry, community, and governmental bodies to protect your organization's reputation, ensure fairness, open opportunities, and protect against threats outside your own control.

Top 3 things to work on this year (development activity)	% complete
1.	
2.	
3.	

Appendix B: How the Standards Were Developed

Finalized in 2017 after five years of research and testing, The General Management Index was created by Derrick Van Mell (BA, MBA, MA-English) and Robert Van Mell (BA, MBA, and MS-Computer Science). It was piloted with the United States Small Business Administration and made public in 2018, and it has been tested with small and large organizations in almost every sector. It is overseen by The Center for Management Terms & Practices.

The Center applies strict editorial guidelines to selecttion of the two to six Approved Resources for each management term in The Index. The guidelines are on the About page at www.theindex.net. Google Trends continues to be a useful tool in researching what management terms are in common use on the internet over the past five years. For example, running Compare for "human resources" and "personnel" revealed that the prevalence of even these basic terms differs globally.

The Pledge of Managerial Power is derived from one of the author's blog posts, "Good Boss Bad Boss." The reaction from a global LinkedIn audience suggested the idea get codified. The Milwaukee Model arose from discussions with the staff of Executive Programs at the Lubar College of Business about the need for a plain-English summary of the skills and knowledge managers need.

All the standards and the tools were tested and refined by application with hundreds of managers at every level in many different sectors. Members of The Center for Management Terms & Practices, the hosting standards body, comment on all these issues at their Best Practice Workgroup meetings.

Appendix C: Management Community Reading List

People who have taken up management as a calling know it's a limitless topic. They'll naturally want to know how to learn and share ideas with like-minded people.

There are, however, few books for management generalists, people who need to see how all the technical and personal aspects of management work together (see the Milwaukee Model). Most management books are about single issues, celebrity CEOs, startling failures, generalities about leadership, or getting rich quickly. There's no standard textbook used in MBA programs.

These four books are well-written, time-tested, and lend themselves to group discussion one chapter at a time.

Street Smarts (originally *The Knack*). Norm Brodsky and Bo Burlingham.

> The commonsense knack for focusing on what's important lets managers succeed time after time. There's no jargon or formula here, but a sensibly structured set of stories. His advice includes running your Gross Margin numbers by hand, to get a feel for this critical ratio.

How to Win Friends and Influence People. Dale Carnegie.

> Written before everyone was a psychoanalyst, this is the book for learning to get along with colleagues, bosses, and staff. It's a collection of stories and anecdotes, and the 1930s writing style is charming. Who wouldn't read "Part One: Fundamental Techniques in Handling People?"

Managing the Professional Services Firm. David Maister.

> Maister was a professor at the Harvard Business School but writes plainly. He consulted with some of the world's largest service firms, but the ideas apply to any organization. Maister focuses on what's essential, using simple examples and math to drive his points home.

Working. Studs Turkel.

> I gave this book to both of my kids when they were in middle school. In 100 interviews, from car hops to corporate executives, Turkel draws out people about what they love and hate about their work. The first interview, with a stone mason, makes plain that meaning comes from the work, not pay or perks.

Grow through community. Dedicated managers need a community of peers from whom to learn and who can be a resource, a sounding board, and a well of moral support. The Center for Management Terms & Practices hosts Best Practice Workgroups, for those who like a structured, intensive, and facilitated approach to learning.

Appendix D: Image Attributions

MUSIC ON THE COVER
Fugue in A-flat Major by J.S. Bach. Public domain.

ATOMS & ORCHESTRAS
Periodic table: licensed from iStock
Musical score: "Grand Battle Sinfonia" by Beethoven. Public domain. https://tinyurl.com/45z9bdyb

THE VALUE OF MANAGEMENT STANDARDS
Train wreck photo: "Montparnasse derailment" by Levy & fils. Public domain. https://tinyurl.com/wz4p8mun
Passing baton photo: licensed from iStock

THE ETHICAL STANDARD
Lego seahorse: author photo

THE TECHNICAL STANDARD
Smartphone cords photo: "USB cable type C blue Bbackground" by user3802032 on Freepik
Compass graphic: "Modern compass icon" by macrovector on Freepik

THE DEVELOPMENTAL STANDARD
Greta Thunberg: By European Parliament - This file has been extracted from another file, CC BY 2.0. https://tinyurl.com/3bphm9dp
Child playing sheet music: licensed from iStock
Girl on diving board: licensed from iStock

THE TOOLKIT
Images of the four management tools by author
Old electric drill: no data on author. Public domain
Overhead image of meeting (also Chap. VIII): licensed from iStock
General Patton: "General George S. Patton in command of US forces on Sicily." No data. Wikipedia Commons. Public domain
Runners at finish line: licensed from iStock

THE PROMISE AND REWARDS OF SERVICE
Yoda: "Dereck Hard Yoda Little Reality 2016" by Honza Nedoma licensed under CC BY-SA 4.0. https://tinyurl.com/ycks4k54
MC Escher sphere: M.C. Escher. Public domain
Mona Lisa: Leonardo da Vinci, Public domain, via Wikimedia Commons
Globe graphic: licensed from iStock

TRIAL & IMPLEMENTATION
Disposable pen: author photo
Overhead image of meeting: see above

www.ingramcontent.com/pod-product-compliance
Lightning Source LLC
LaVergne TN
LVHW070217110826
845147LV00003B/596

* 9 7 8 0 9 7 7 0 9 1 4 4 7 *